PUPCAKES

35 delicious and healthy recipes for dogs

Stephanie Mehanna
In association with

The Canine Cookie Company Ltd.

hamlyn

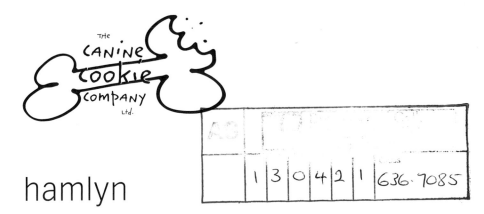

First published in Great Britain in 2007 by Hamlyn,
a division of Octopus Publishing Group Ltd
2–4 Heron Quays, London E14 4JP

ISBN-13: 978-0-600-61657-3
ISBN-10: 0-600-61657-6

A CIP catalogue record of this book is available from the British Library.

Printed and bound in China

10 9 8 7 6 5 4 3 2 1

Publisher's note

The advice given in this book should not be used as a substitute for that of a veterinary surgeon. The techniques, ideas and suggestions are to be used at the reader's sole discretion and risk. No dogs were harmed in making this book.

Recipes Notes

- Standard level spoon measurement are used in all recipes: 1 tablespoon = one 15 ml spoon; 1 teaspoon = one 5 ml spoon.
- Both imperial and metric measurements have been given in all recipes. Use one set of measurements only and not a mixture of both.
- Fresh herbs should be used unless otherwise stated. If unavailable use dried herbs as an alternative but halve the quantities stated.
- Ovens should be preheated to the specific temperature – if using a fan-assisted oven, follow manufacturer's instructions for adjusting the time and the temperature.
- Many vets recommend that you do not feed raw or lightly cooked eggs to your dog due to the risk of salmonella. This book contains dishes made with raw or lightly cooked eggs. It is prudent for more vulnerable dogs, such as pregnant and nursing bitches, sick or elderly dogs and puppies, to avoid uncooked or lightly cooked dishes made with eggs. Once prepared these dishes should be kept refrigerated and used promptly.

Contents

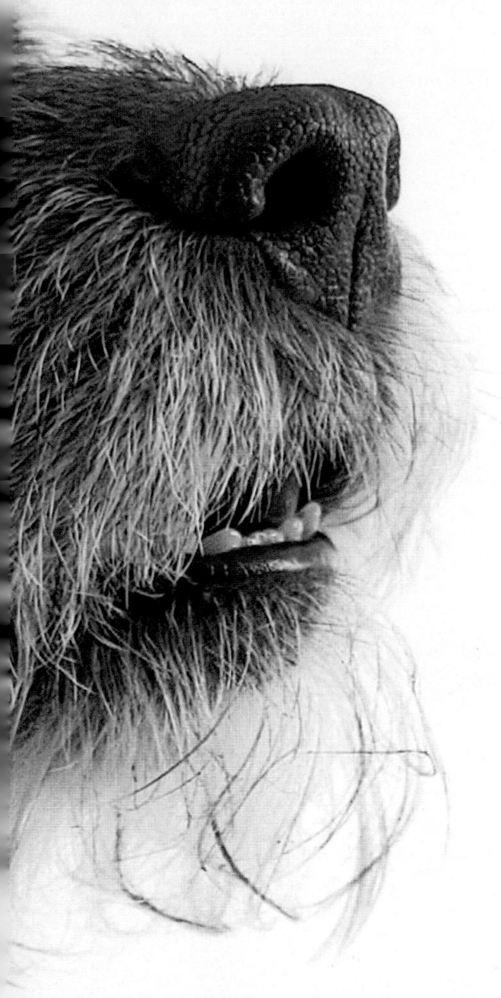

Introduction

Welcome to the idea of cooking for your dog! Whether you've dabbled with a recipe or two for your Chihuahua, rustled up a hearty three-course meal for your Great Dane, or never before attempted to do more than open a bag of dog food, this book is for you *and* your dog.

Why bake? Cooking is an act of love; it nurtures and bonds. No one can cook for your dog better than you, regardless of your culinary skills or nutritional know-how. You know his likes and dislikes; you understand what he needs, his age, his weight and his history. Your dog won't notice if you slightly overcook a dish, replace one ingredient for another or forget to add a herb or two. He'll love you and your cooking because he knows you do it just for him.

In the wild, dogs scavenged for natural treats. Fruit, berries, nuts, even herbs found their way into the canine diet, so add flavour and texture to your dog's meals with a healthy hand-baked treat.

Cooking for your dog is about having fun. Think of it as quality time together trying out new tastes and smells. These recipes are just a starting point – add or change ingredients according to your dog's preferences and what is good for him to eat. These homemade treats don't have the high fat and sugar content present in some commercial ones, so you can be sure you are preparing healthy treats for your dog. Although too many treats can cause weight gain, the occasional healthy, low-fat reward won't unbalance his diet. The recipes in this book are formulated to give your dog a healthy treat, not to replace his main meal of the day.

Homemade treats are a great way to reward good behaviour, too. Pop a small bag of Training Tidbits in your pocket for your next walk. Experiment and learn what your dog really likes, then have fun with different flavours and shapes. Your dog will no doubt be happy to taste-test any new dish you choose to bake!

This book isn't about producing a 'complete' balanced meal plan for your dog. Here, you'll learn how to use human-grade quality ingredients to bake healthy and tasty treats to nurture and protect your pet.

The Basics of Canine Nutrition

Before you begin baking, it's important to gain an understanding of general canine nutrition. Protein, fat, carbohydrate, vitamins, minerals and water are essential for a balanced diet. The amount of each nutrient your dog needs depends on his age, breed and weight, so always discuss your feeding pattern and choice of food for your dog with your vet.

Protein is the most important component in your dog's diet. It helps him grow, develop muscles and tendons, produce healthy hair and nails, build a stable immune system and create the right amount of hormones.

A 'complete' protein comprises 20 different essential and non-essential amino acids. Complete proteins only come from animal sources, such as lean meat and eggs. Incomplete proteins, such as wheat, corn and soybean, don't supply all the essential amino acids so they are not so beneficial. Your dog's diet should contain mostly complete proteins: don't buy a dog food where the primary ingredient is wheat or corn gluten as he may find it difficult to digest.

Adult dogs require, on average, a minimum of 18 per cent protein in their diet. Puppies and pregnant bitches require a minimum of 22 per cent, while working dogs may require more.

Carbohydrates play a vital role in providing your dog with energy and ensuring cells function properly, including muscle and brain cells. They often serve as a fibre to help in the formation of healthy faeces and are also useful in aiding digestion of other nutrients such as fats.

Simple carbohydrates are the sugars found in fruits, honey and cornsyrup. These are easy for the body to break down into glucose, which is used as energy. Complex carbohydrates include the starches found in some vegetables, grains, rice, bread and pasta. These take longer to break down and convert into glucose. They are more satisfying for your dog, as the energy is released slowly and for a longer time. All carbohydrates can be converted into and stored as fat in the body if they are not used. Up to 50 per cent of a healthy adults dog's diet can be made up of complex carbohydrates.

Fibre in your dog's food comes from cellulose, a complex carbohydrate that is not so easy to break down and is found in plant stems and leaves. It usually passes straight through the digestive system and has no nutritional value but provides bulk and a feeling of fullness. The correct amount of fibre is important for the efficient functioning of your dog's digestive system. Regular monitoring of his faeces will ensure there is not too much or too little fibre in your dog's diet: they should be firm but bulky and moist. A healthy adult dog requires, on average, a minimum of 2.5 to 4.5 per cent fibre in their diet.

Fat often gets a bad press, but in the canine diet it is essential for providing energy. It also helps keep your dog's skin supple and coat healthy. Too much, however, causes obesity and conditions such as pancreatitis, so monitor his fat intake carefully and make sure he gets lots of exercise.

Fats contain fatty acids, including the vitally important omega-6 which helps keep his paw pads and nose leather supple. Good sources of omega-6 may be found in lean chicken, beef and safflower oil. Omega-3 is another useful fatty acid. It reduces stiffness and inflammation and has been found to be effective when treating arthritis. Fish oils provide natural omega-3 in the diet.

Adult dogs, on average, require a minimum of 5 per cent fat in their diet. Puppies and pregnant bitches need a minimum of 8 per cent. Only working dogs may require more.

Vitamins are essential to your dog's health, and there are 14 different types that he needs. Vitamins aid growth and promote the chemical reactions required to help his digestive system absorb the nutrients from his food. They can be found in fruits, vegetables, meat and fish. There are two types: fat-soluble and water-soluble vitamins.

Fat-soluble vitamins (A, D, E and K) are stored in his body fat, ready to be used. If he is fed a balanced diet he should get enough fat-soluble vitamins without the need to supplement.

Water-soluble vitamins (C, B1, B2, B6, B12, biotin, choline, folic acid, niacin and pantothenic acid) are all needed on a daily basis – he can't store them. If he is fed a balanced diet he will receive the required amounts without supplements. However, if you feel your dog needs additional vitamins, discuss this with your vet.

Water makes up two-thirds of your dog's body weight. Dogs lose water via urine, faeces, panting and drooling. They can easily become dehydrated, which can be dangerous, so always make sure fresh water is available for your dog.

Minerals help activate the enzymes that control digestion, metabolism and the production of healthy blood cells. They should be present in sufficient quantities if your dog's diet contains good-quality meat, poultry, fish, organ meat, egg or bonemeal. The minerals he requires in his diet include calcium, magnesium, phosphorus, sulphur, copper, iron, cobalt, iodine, manganese, selenium and zinc.

Dogs on Special Diets

Try the following recipes if your dog is on a special diet or has special needs. If you are unsure whether a dish is suitable, show your vet the recipe and ask for advice.

Wheat allergy All the recipes use wheat- and gluten-free flour, available from good health food shops, as wheat allergies are common among dogs. Some of the recipes don't contain any flour or grains, including Box-er Chocolates (see page 82).

Feeling under the weather If your dog has been sick or is recovering from an illness, try Tummy-rub Tea (see page 88). Always consult your vet if your dog continues to vomit or have diarrhoea.

Piling on the pounds If your dog is overweight, try providing more fibre and less protein. Most of our treats are low in fat, particularly the Fat Busters (see page 92).

STOP AND HEEL!

Always avoid the following foods. Some are poisonous, some can cause an allergic reaction, while others just aren't good for your dog.

INGREDIENT	POTENTIAL REACTION
Alcohol	Very toxic to dogs. Can cause vomiting and in severe cases coma.
Artificial sweeteners	Xylitol is used in sugarless gum and some sweets. Can cause a sudden drop in blood sugar levels, resulting in depression and loss of coordination.
Avocado	Contain a toxic component called persin that can damage a dog's heart and lungs. It is also high in fat and can cause stomach upsets.
Chocolate	Contains theobromine or theophylline, which can stem the flow of blood to the brain.
Coffee, tea and cocoa	Contain theobromine and caffeine that can cause vomiting and diarrhoea.
Cooked bones	Raw bones are nutritious for your dog, but cooked bones can splinter and lodge in the throat or stomach.
Grapes and raisins	Contain a toxin that can damage the kidneys of dogs.
Hops	Dogs can go into shock if they digest hops used by home brewers. Dispose of hops very carefully.
Macadamia nuts	Create weakness and stiffness in the legs by attacking the nervous system.
Mouldy food	Can contain multiple toxins that cause vomiting and diarrhoea.

INGREDIENT	POTENTIAL REACTION
Mushrooms	Can contain toxins that affect the nervous system and in severe cases cause shock.
Onions	Can cause anaemia and even kidney failure. Just one is enough to cause harm. Garlic and chives, also members of the *Allium* family, can be eaten in small quantities without causing any harm to your dog.
Potato, tomato and rhubarb stems/leaves	Contain oxalates, which can upset the digestive system and urinary tract.
Raw eggs	There is a small risk of salmonella. They also contain an enzyme that can reduce the absorption of biotin. Can be fed to a healthy dog occasionally.
Raw fish	Too much can lead to a deficiency in thiamine, resulting in loss of appetite and seizures. Only feed occasionally and sprinkle with brewer's yeast, a great source of thiamine.
Synthetic colourings	Can contain artificial additives. For natural colourings, try beetroot juice, carrots and crushed tomatoes.
Tobacco	Contains nicotine that can affect the nervous and digestive systems. This can result in an increased heart rate and physical collapse.
Yeast dough	If eaten raw, it can expand in the stomach causing pain and possible rupture.

Found a flea? If your dog suffers flea infestations, try Flea-fighters (see page 86). Fleas hate the smell of garlic!

Barkin' breath If your dog suffers from bad breath, try After-dinner Mints (see page 60). The fresh mint, parsley and activated charcoal will bring a little freshness to his mouth.

Vegetarian If your dog is following a vegetarian diet, tempt him with Pupp-eroni Pizza (see page 52) or Tail Twists (see page 14).

Kidney disease It is thought that a low-protein diet can help to manage kidney disease and aid recovery. Try Salivating Sushi Snacks (see page 41), using lamb as the filling rather than chicken hearts or kidneys.

Senior dogs A low-protein and low-sodium diet is also recommended for older dogs as it reduces the wear and tear on vital organs. Offer Mutts de la Mer (see page 33) to your faithful old companion.

Heart disease A low-sodium diet can help manage heart disease in dogs. Many commercial foods and treats are high in sodium and should be avoided. *Never add salt to your dog's diet.* Try Pick-me-up Punch (see page 89), which also includes flaxseed. Flaxseed contains omega-3 fatty acids, which can help regulate hormones in dogs with heart disease.

The Paw-fect Pantry

Most of the ingredients in this book can be found in a local grocery store. Buying locally means your meat and vegetables are fresher and therefore contain higher levels of vitamins and minerals. Items such as blackstrap molasses and wheat- and gluten-free flour, bread and pasta are available from health food shops.

Kitchen Safety

All treats should be kept in an airtight container. Refrigerate meat- and cheese-based treats and use within a few days. Recipes such as Chicken Soup (see page 40), Canine's Curry with Bark-mati rice (see page 54) and Pasta Bark Slice (see page 50) can be frozen in portions and defrosted to order.

Always buy fresh meat and poultry from a reputable supplier, preferably a local butcher who can trim fat and unwanted bones for you. Refrigerate until required. Store cooked and uncooked meat separately in the refrigerator and always cover.

If you are making meat or poultry treats to feed raw, ensure that once the recipe is prepared it is stored in the refrigerator or preferably the freezer. Only take out what you need and use immediately. If you need to transport frozen meat, use a cool bag and feed within 2–3 hours. Do not let treats defrost; feed frozen to ensure freshness. Your dog won't mind whether his treats are frozen or not!

How Much and How Often?

Some of the recipes in this book are just for celebrations, others are intended as an occasional treat. All recipes are complementary; they are treats and should not be fed in place of a complete balanced diet. Recipes such as Chicken Soup (see page 40) can be added daily as a meal topper and will provide flavour and essential nutrients, particularly if you feed your dog on dry biscuits.

When feeding treats, reduce your dog's basic food ration to compensate so he still gets the same total weight of food each day.

Afternoon Tea and Tails

Whether it's just tea for two or a pooch paw-ty these tempting treats will make sure you are leader of the pack!

Catty-cakes

These yummy, moist pupcakes are bursting with tasty banana and peanut butter and are full of grrrreat goodness for your dog.

1 Mix all the cake ingredients together in a large bowl until well combined. Divide the mixture evenly between 20 individual paper baking cases.

2 Bake in a preheated oven, 160°C (325°F), Gas Mark 3, for 15–20 minutes until they are well risen and spring back when pressed with a fingertip. Insert a knife into one of the cakes: if it comes out clean, they are cooked. Remove the cakes from the oven and leave them to cool.

3 To make the frosting to decorate the cakes, combine the cream cheese or quark, peanut butter and oil and beat until fluffy. Transfer the frosting to a piping bag fitted with a thin nozzle and decorate each cake with a cat's face. Use the cherry pieces to make the nose and eyes. Catty-cakes can be stored in the refrigerator for up to 3 days, or in the freezer for up to 3 months.

Makes 20
Preparation time: 15 minutes
Cooking time: 15–20 minutes

375 g (12 oz) wheat- and gluten-free flour
300 ml (½ pint) semi-skimmed milk
250 g (8 oz) peanut butter (no added salt or sugar)
2 eggs
1 banana, mashed
4 tablespoons honey
4 tablespoons vegetable oil
1 teaspoon baking powder
1 teaspoon baking soda
1 teaspoon pure vanilla extract

To decorate:
250 g (8 oz) low-fat cream cheese or quark
125 g (4 oz) peanut butter (no added salt or sugar)
4 tablespoons olive oil
10 glacé cherries, cut into pieces

Tail Twists

Cheesy twists are perfect for a poochie party! The flaxseed adds a crunchy, nutty flavour and is rich in essential fatty acids and fibre, helping to maintain a healthy immune system.

Makes 32–34
Preparation time: 15 minutes
Cooking time: 30–35 minutes

300 g (10 oz) wheat- and gluten-free flour
50 g (2 oz) low-fat Cheddar cheese, grated
25 g (1 oz) low-fat Parmesan cheese, grated
1 tablespoon chopped thyme
2 tablespoons milled flaxseed
125 ml (4 fl oz) olive oil
100 ml (3½ fl oz) cold water

1 Mix the flour, cheeses, thyme and flaxseed in a large bowl. Add the oil and combine. Add the water a little at a time until the mixture forms a firm dough.

2 Knead the dough on a lightly floured surface and divide into 3.5-cm (1½-inch) balls. Roll out each ball into a 15-cm (6-inch) sausage. Pat lightly with the rolling pin to flatten, then hold both ends and twist in opposite directions.

3 Place the twists on a greased baking sheet, 1 cm (½ inch) apart. Bake in a preheated oven, 160°C (325°C), Gas Mark 3, for 30–35 minutes or until golden-brown in colour. Remove from the oven and leave the twists to cool on the baking sheet. The twists will keep for 7–10 days in an airtight tin or container.

Tips'n'Tails

Whisk 2 spoonfuls of low-fat cottage cheese with a spoonful of smooth, low salt and sugar peanut butter for a mouth-watering dip, paw-fect to dip your Tail Twists in! Peanut butter is packed with vitamins A and E, folic acid, zinc, calcium, magnesium, iron and fibre. It's also quite high in fat, so don't leave the open jar within easy reach of your hungry hound!

Turkey and Cheese Muffins

Invite your dog's pals over for a special afternoon tea and serve up these yummy muffins as mouth-watering treats.

Makes 12–15
Preparation time: 15 minutes
Cooking time: 20–25 minutes

300 g (10 oz) wheat- and gluten-free flour
1 teaspoon baking powder
1 teaspoon baking soda
2 turkey bacon rashers, grilled and chopped
100 g (3½ oz) low-fat Cheddar cheese, grated
1 egg, beaten
4 tablespoons olive oil
150 ml (¼ pint) cold water

1 Grease a nonstick muffin tray with olive oil. Mix the flour, baking powder, baking soda, turkey and cheese in a large mixing bowl. Add the egg and olive oil and stir to combine. Add the cold water, a little at a time, until you have a runny batter. Use a ladle to divide the mixture between the muffin cups, leaving a little room at the top for the mixture to expand.

2 Bake in a preheated oven, 180°C (350°F), Gas Mark 4, for 20–25 minutes or until golden brown. Transfer to a wire rack to cool. Store the muffins in an airtight container in the refrigerator for up to 3 days.

Chicken and Tarragon Bone Biscuits

Crunchy chicken-lickin' bones, flavoured with tarragon. Light and yummy, these tasty bones make a great snack before bedtime, or a satisfying mid-afternoon treat.

1 To make the chicken broth, place the chicken in a small saucepan with the measured water. Bring to the boil and simmer for 15 minutes until the chicken is cooked through. Remove the chicken from the water and set aside to cool. Reserve the broth and finely shred the cooled chicken.

2 In a large bowl, mix the flour, wheat germ, egg, oil and tarragon until combined. Add the chicken and stir into the mixture.

3 Slowly add 175 ml (6 fl oz) of the reserved chicken broth to make a dough. Knead the dough on a lightly floured surface until it is firm, then roll out to 1 cm (½ inch) thick. Cut out shapes with a bone-shaped cookie cutter.

4 Place the bones on a greased baking sheet, 1 cm (½ inch) apart, and brush with beaten egg. Bake in a preheated oven, 160°C (325°F), Gas Mark 3, for 25–30 minutes. When ready, the cookies should be firm to the touch. Remove the cookies from the oven and allow them to cool and harden for 1–2 hours. Store any leftover bones in the refrigerator for up to 2 weeks.

Makes 45–50
Preparation time: 20 minutes, plus hardening
Cooking time: 40–45 minutes

250 g (8 oz) wholemeal wheat- and gluten-free flour
50 g (2 oz) wheat germ
1 egg, beaten, plus extra for brushing
125 ml (4 fl oz) olive oil
1 tablespoon dried tarragon

For the broth:
375 g (12 oz) boneless skinless chicken thighs, chopped
500 ml (17 fl oz) cold water

Tips'n'Tails

Doughs made with wheat- and gluten-free flour are not always firm enough to be rolled out. If your dog doesn't have an allergy use standard plain flour instead. Alternatively, place spoonfuls of dough on the baking tray and spread out with the back of the spoon to form the cookies.

Apple and Cinnamon Lollipups

These sweet apple and cinnamon lollipups are the perfect treat for the well-behaved pooch.

Makes 10–15
Preparation time: 20 minutes, plus hardening
Cooking time: 15–20 minutes

2 apples, chopped
approximately 50 ml (2 fl oz) water
500 g (1 lb) wheat- and gluten-free flour
2 eggs, beaten, plus extra to glaze
150 ml (¼ pint) olive oil
50 g (2 oz) wheat germ
4 tablespoons honey
1½ tablespoons ground cinnamon
10–15 rawhide chew sticks

For the frosting:
125 g (4 oz) low-fat cream cheese
4 tablespoons olive oil
1 tablespoon pure vanilla extract

For the piping:
125 g (4 oz) low-fat cream cheese
4 tablespoons olive oil
8 tablespoons carob powder

1 Purée the apples in a food processor or blender with the water. Mix the apple purée with the flour, eggs, oil, wheat germ, honey and cinnamon in a large bowl, adding a little more water if the dough is too dry.

2 Knead the dough on a lightly floured surface and roll out to 5 mm (¼ inch) thick. Cut out the lollipup shapes with a paw-shaped cookie cutter or use an upturned glass to cut 7-cm (3-inch) discs from the dough. Make sure you cut an even number of discs. Brush each cookie with beaten egg and sprinkle with additional cinnamon, if desired. Place one cookie on top of another, with egg-brushed sides together. Pinch the edges together. Pair up the remaining discs in the same way.

3 Place the cookies on a greased baking sheet, 1 cm (½ inch) apart. Bake in a preheated oven, 150°C (300°C), Gas Mark 2, for 15–20 minutes.

4 Make a 1-cm (½-inch) wide incision in between the 2 cookie layers with a small knife, and insert ⅓ of the length of a rawhide stick between the cookies. Wrap the exposed rawhide in baking foil. Repeat with the remaining doggie lollipups, then return them to the oven. Turn the oven off, and let the lollipups cool and harden in the oven for 1–2 hours.

5 For the frosting, mix all the frosting ingredients together and beat until fluffy. Spread on the cookies. For the carob piping, mix all the ingredients until well combined. Pour into a piping bag fitted with a fine nozzle, then pipe your chosen design on to the lollipups. Stored in the refrigerator for up to 3 days.

Training Tidbits

They say you can't teach an old dog new tricks. Well whoever said that hadn't just home-baked a batch of these yummy rewards. They are doggie-licious!

Liver Bait Fudge

Liver Bait is the perfect reward for the perfectly behaved pooch. Use these nutritious liver and turkey bacon bites as a treat when training, at agility class, or just because...

Makes 96
Preparation time: 15 minutes
Cooking time: 30–35 minutes

400 g (13 oz) chickens' or lambs' liver
300 ml (½ pint) cold water
400 g (13 oz) wheat- and gluten-free flour
½ teaspoon chopped garlic
4 turkey bacon rashers, grilled and chopped
1 egg
65 ml (2½ fl oz) olive oil

1 Liquidize the liver and measured water in a food processor or blender. Transfer to a large bowl, add the flour, garlic, turkey bacon, egg and olive oil, and mix with a spoon until it forms a smooth paste.

2 Pour the ingredients into a 18 x 28-cm (7 x 11-inch) shallow baking tin lined with greased greaseproof paper. Cook in a preheated oven, 180°C (350°F), Gas Mark 4, for 30–35 minutes. Prick with a fork halfway through cooking to release the air. Check it is cooked through by inserting a knife. If the knife comes out clean, it is ready. Otherwise, return to the oven for 2–3 more minutes. Transfer to a wire rack to cool.

3 Cut into 2.5-cm (1-inch) cubes using a sharp knife. Place the liver bait cubes into small resealable freezer bags and freeze until required. Defrost a bag in the refrigerator before your next training session.

Tips'n'Tails

Liver Bait Fudge should be consumed on the day of defrosting. It will keep in the freezer for up to 1 month. Don't refreeze once defrosted.

Jumping for Jerky

Your dog will be jumping for joy at the taste of these natural meaty treats. Perfect for taking on long walks, when camping or on holiday.

Makes 20–40 (depending on thickness)
Preparation time: 10 minutes, plus marinating
Cooking time: 4–5 hours

50 ml (2 fl oz) blackstrap molasses
½ teaspoon chopped garlic
1 tablespoon dried rosemary
500 g (1 lb) lamb or venison, sliced into thin strips along the grain with fat removed

1 Combine the molasses, garlic and rosemary in a large bowl. Add the meat and stir, making sure it is all covered with the marinade. Leave to marinate for 1–2 hours in the refrigerator.

2 Line a baking sheet with foil and place a wire rack on top. Lay the marinated meat strips on the wire rack and brush with the remaining marinade.

3 Cook in a preheated oven, 110°C (225°F), Gas Mark ¼, for 4–5 hours. Remove the baking sheet from the oven, then leave the jerky to cool. Store for up to 5–7 days in an airtight container in the refrigerator.

Tips'n'Tails

Molasses is high in vitamins and minerals, including iron and calcium. Just 1 tablespoon of blackstrap molasses has the same iron content as an average steak. Using molasses is a great way to add a little natural sweetness and goodness to your treats.

Magic Muttballs

These muttballs really are magic. Watch your dog perform the perfect 'sit' for one of these tasty balls of goodness.

Makes 50
Preparation time: 15 minutes
Cooking time: 15–20 minutes

500 g (1 lb) minced rabbit or chicken
150 g (5 oz) dried breadcrumbs, made with wheat- and gluten-free bread
1 tablespoon dried oregano
1 egg

1 Mix all the ingredients in a large bowl. Roll into 2.5-cm (1-inch) balls and place on a greased baking sheet.

2 Bake in a preheated oven, 180°C (350°F), Gas Mark 4, for 15–20 minutes or until golden brown. Remove the balls from the oven and leave them to cool.

3 Transfer to an airtight container and store in the refrigerator. Alternatively, place in resealable freezer bags and freeze for up to 6 weeks until required. It's fine for your dog to eat the muttballs frozen.

Tips'n'Tails

After making the balls, roll them in 25 g (1 oz) of breadcrumbs (additional) and freeze one layer at a time in small freezer bags or airtight containers. Remove frozen treats as required: your dog won't mind if they are frozen. Try not to let the frozen balls defrost during travel as this could affect their stability. If you feed your dog a raw diet, then it is fine to also make these treats raw.

Magnificent Muffins

Good behaviour deserves a little recognition in the form of a tasty treat. When your best friend has been especially well behaved, reward him or her with a doggie-licious muffin that's packed with goodness.

Makes 15–18
Preparation time: 15 minutes
Cooking time: 20–25 minutes

300 g (10 oz) wheat- and gluten-free flour
1 teaspoon baking powder
1 teaspoon baking soda
2 tablespoons carob powder
½ teaspoon ground cinnamon
100 g (3½ oz) pumpkin, cooked and mashed
1 tablespoon honey
1 egg, beaten
3 tablespoons olive oil, plus extra for greasing
200 ml (7 fl oz) cold water

1 Mix all the dry ingredients with the pumpkin and the honey in a large mixing bowl. Stir in the egg and the olive oil, then add the measured water, a little at a time, until you have a runny batter. Grease a nonstick muffin or bun tray with olive oil. Fill the muffin cups with the batter, leaving a little room at the top for the mixture to expand.

2 Bake in a preheated oven, 180°C (350°F), Gas Mark 4, for 20–25 minutes or until golden brown. Test if the muffins are ready by inserting a toothpick or skewer. If it comes out clean, they are ready. Transfer to a wire rack and leave to cool. Store the muffins in an airtight container in the refrigerator for up to 1 week.

Tips'n'Tails

Pumpkin is low in fat and high in fibre. It provides a good source of potassium and beta-carotene, which gives pumpkin and carrots their orange colour. It helps to kick-start the immune system and its antioxidant properties may help prevent cancer and other diseases.

Mutts de la Mer

Tasty, fishy patties made with tuna, salmon and quinoa. Packed full of goodness, these treats promote healthy skin and coat. Quinoa is a complete protein, containing all eight essential amino acids. It is also rich in minerals and omega oils and is gluten free.

1 Mix all the ingredients in a large bowl until combined. Scoop out large teaspoons of the mixture and roll it in your hands to form 3.5-cm (1½-inch) balls – or spoon off small handfuls and mould into bone-shaped patties and balls. Place on to a baking sheet lined with greaseproof paper.

2 Bake in a preheated oven, 200°C (400°F), Gas Mark 6, for 15–20 minutes until golden. Transfer to a wire rack to cool.

3 Place in small resealable freezer bags and freeze until required. Defrost at room temperature and use on the same day. The patties will keep in the freezer for up to 3 weeks.

Makes 30–40
Preparation time: 10 minutes
Cooking time: 15–20 minutes

250 g (8 oz) cooked quinoa
400 g (13 oz) canned red salmon, well drained
150 g (5 oz) canned tuna, well drained
75 ml (3 fl oz) blackstrap molasses
50 g (2 oz) wheat- and gluten-free flour
1 egg, beaten

Tips'n'Tails

You can substitute canned tuna and salmon for fresh fish, but make sure it is canned in spring water and not brine or oil, and that you remove all the bones. Sprinkle the fish with 1 teaspoon of brewer's yeast or Marmite, which is fantastic for aiding digestion. It tastes good too!

Fruity Furrballs

This is our Irish Setter Alfie's favourite treat. Healthy and simple, dried fruit is a natural alternative to low-quality manufactured treats. If you have a very small dog, cut the apple rings in half before dipping in carob.

Makes 20–30
Preparation time: 15 minutes

150 g (5 oz) carob chips or carob bar, broken into small pieces
1 tablespoon pure vanilla extract
250 g (8 oz) naturally dried apricots, apple rings and bananas (non-sulphur varieties)
50 g (2 oz) blanched almonds, chopped

1 Place the carob in a heatproof glass bowl. Set the bowl over a saucepan of lightly simmering water and heat until the carob has melted. Stir in the vanilla extract.

2 Use a fork to dip each piece of dried fruit into the carob so half of the fruit is coated. Then dip into the chopped nuts and place on greaseproof paper.

3 Leave to set for 20 minutes. Transfer to an airtight container and chill until hard. Fruity Furrballs will keep for up to 4 weeks in the refrigerator.

Tips'n'Tails

Carob is a safe alternative to chocolate as chocolate is poisonous for dogs. Carob is full of vitamins, including vitamin A, which is necessary for good vision, and vitamins B1 and B2, which aid growth. It is also rich in calcium, phosphate, protein, potassium, iron, silicon and magnesium.

Quick and Easy Entrées

For the dog on the go, these paw-tastic bites are full of goodness and flavour. Pack for a long hike, camping trip or car journey.

Turkey Bake Tempter

Ask your dog to sit for this classic turkey-and-veg meal that's so simple to prepare yet so impressive when cut into bite-sized mini bakes.

Makes 10–12 portions
Preparation time: 10 minutes
Cooking time: 40–45 minutes

- 500 g (1 lb) minced turkey
- 150 g (5 oz) dried breadcrumbs, made from wheat- and gluten-free bread
- 1 egg, beaten
- 1 sweet potato, cooked and mashed
- 150 g (5 oz) carrots, thinly sliced
- 100 g (3½ oz) green beans, thinly sliced
- 1 tablespoon chopped sage
- 3 tablespoons homemade chicken stock or water
- 1 tablespoon brewer's yeast

1 Mix all the ingredients in a large mixing bowl until well combined. Transfer the mixture to a deep 25 x 30-cm (10 x 12-inch) ovenproof dish and level out with the back of a spoon. Bake in a preheated oven, 180°C (350°), Gas Mark 4, for 40–45 minutes until firm. Remove from the oven and leave to cool.

2 Cut the turkey bake into 5-cm (2-inch) squares and store for up to 5 days in an airtight container in the refrigerator. Serve cool or cold as your dog cannot digest hot food and it can cause damage to the lining of his stomach.

Chicken Soup

This chicken and vegetable soup is a great meal-topper for regular dog food. The natural gravy adds flavour without the salt and preservatives found in gravy granules.

Makes 2 litres (3½ pints)
Preparation time: 25 minutes
Cooking time: 25–35 minutes

1 free-range chicken, cut into quarters
2 carrots, sliced
2 litres (3½ pints) cold water
2 tablespoons cornflour, diluted in 100 ml (3½ fl oz) cold water
50 g (2 oz) cabbage, shredded
1 tablespoon dried oregano

1 Place the chicken pieces in a large saucepan with the carrots. Add the measured water and simmer for 20–30 minutes or until the chicken is cooked through. Remove the chicken from the stock and set aside.

2 Bring the stock back to simmering point, add the diluted cornflour and stir until it has thickened. Add the cabbage and oregano and simmer for 5 minutes. Turn the heat off, then leave to cool.

3 Discard the chicken bones and skin, and finely shred the meat. Add to the cooled soup. Transfer to plastic containers and refrigerate for up to 3 days, or freeze for up to 3 months. Serve cold or warmed slightly, but never hot – your dog cannot digest hot food and it can cause damage to his stomach lining.

Tips'n'Tails

Add berries to the soup if your dog has a sweet tooth, or swap the chicken for liver or vegetables. Keep a container in the refrigerator and pour a little over your dog's main meal. For small dogs, use 5 tablespoons of soup with each meal, for medium dogs use 8 tablespoons, and for large dogs use 12 tablespoons.

Salivating Sushi Snacks

Your dog doesn't have to be Japanese to enjoy these novel and nutritious treats. Made with nori, a dried sea vegetable, these sushi snacks are full of nutritious minerals.

Makes 15
Preparation time: 30 minutes
Cooking time: 3 minutes

2 carrots, cut lengthways into thin strips
100 g (3½ oz) lamb heart or kidneys, trimmed and cut into strips
3 sheets of Japanese sushi nori
200 g (7 oz) short-grain sticky rice, cooked and cooled
3 tablespoons natural tomato purée
¼ cucumber, cut lengthways into thin strips

1 Boil the carrot strips for 2 minutes, remove from the water, rinse and set aside to cool. Poach the strips of kidney or heart in the boiling water for 1 minute to seal, then set aside to cool.

2 Place 1 sheet of nori on a bamboo sushi mat or piece of greaseproof paper. Spread half the rice on to the nori, leaving a 1-cm (½-inch) bare edge at the top and bottom. Don't overfill with rice.

3 Spread half the tomato purée along the centre of the rice, moving from left to right. Place half the carrot and cucumber on top of the tomato purée. Place some strips of heart or kidney on either side of the vegetables.

4 Gently roll up the sushi, starting with the edge nearest to you. Pull the edge of the sushi mat or greaseproof paper back as you go so it doesn't get rolled up with the sushi. When you get to the other edge of the sushi sheet, wet the nori with a pastry brush dipped in cold water and continuing rolling to seal. Repeat with the other sheet of nori and the remaining filling ingredients.

5 Cut the sushi rolls with a sharp, moistened knife into 3.5-cm (1½-inch) pieces. Transfer to an airtight container and refrigerate. Use on the same day.

Tips'n'Tails

Nori seaweed is rich in vitamins, including C and B12, and in minerals and trace minerals. The most important is iodine, essential for regulating your dog's metabolism and energy levels, but can be harmful in large quantities. Nori contains high levels of iodine, so don't feed this treat to him on a daily basis.

Paw-fect Pâté

This is a lighter take on the more traditional pâté. Oily fish provides a healthy alternative to meat-based treats, while live natural yogurt helps to maintain a healthy gut.

1 Place the mackerel in a large bowl and mash with a fork or process in a food processor. Add the cheese, yogurt and parsley and mix until well combined.

2 Transfer to an airtight container and refrigerate until needed. Use as a healthy, tasty topping for your dog's main meal of the day. It will keep in the refrigerator for up to 2–3 days. Bring each portion up to room temperature (for about 10 minutes) before serving.

Makes 8 portions
Preparation time: 15 minutes

250 g (8 oz) smoked mackerel fillets, skinned
200 g (7 oz) low-fat cream cheese
200 g (7 oz) low-fat live natural yogurt
15 g (½ oz) parsley, chopped

Tips'n'Tails

This mackerel pâté has all the goodness you would expect from an oily fish. It also contains vitamin B6, which is essential in the formation of red blood cells and helps your dog to digest protein. Smoked mackerel can be salty, so only feed this dish to your dog as a special treat in small quantities.

Hearty Hound Mains

For a tasty change from your dog's regular chow, cook up his favourite dish and watch him beg for more!

Marvellous Muttloaf

This wholesome muttloaf is full of delicious flavours. Your pup won't paws for thought over this meal.

Makes 8–10 portions
Preparation time: 25 minutes
Cooking time: 1–1½ minutes

150 g (5 oz) carrots, finely diced
125 g (4 oz) fresh or frozen peas
500 g (1 lb) minced beef
75 g (3 oz) fresh wholemeal breadcrumbs, made with wheat- and gluten-free bread
2 tablespoons tomato purée
15 g (½ oz) parsley, chopped
2 eggs, beaten
125 g (4 oz) low-fat Parmesan cheese, shaved
3 eggs, hard-boiled and shelled

1 Steam the carrots and peas until just tender and set aside to cool. Mix the minced beef with the breadcrumbs, tomato purée, parsley and beaten eggs until well combined. Stir in the carrots and peas.

2 Roll the mixture into a ball and divide in half. Place half of the mixture in the base of a greased 1-kg (2-lb) loaf tin, pressing firmly down into the corners. Make a slight dip along the the centre.

3 Sprinkle with the shaved Parmesan, then place the boiled eggs in a row down the centre of the tin. Place the remaining mixture on top and press firmly around the sides and on top to completely cover the eggs.

4 Cover with foil and bake on the middle shelf of a preheated oven, 180°C (350°F), Gas Mark 4, for 1–1½ hours. Turn out on to a plate and leave to cool. Cut into slices, sprinkle with chopped parsley and serve. Store any leftover muttloaf in the refrigerator for up to a week.

Tips'n'Tails

Carrots are a great source of vitamin C, benefiting your dog's vision, his heart, skin and lungs. They are also rich in beta-carotene, which helps protect against cancer.

Pasta Bark Slice

This nutritious pasta bake makes a tasty mid-week supper and a welcome change from your dog's regular food.

Makes 8–10 portions
Preparation time: 20 minutes
Cooking time: 15–20 minutes

250 g (8 oz) cooked wheat- and gluten-free pasta, chopped
200 g (7 oz) low-fat cottage cheese
200 g (7 oz) low-fat natural yogurt
5 basil leaves, chopped
50 g (2 oz) French beans, topped, tailed and finely chopped
200 g (7 oz) cooked boneless, skinless rabbit or chicken
2 tablespoons olive oil
2 tablespoons grated low-fat Parmesan cheese

1 Mix all the ingredients, except the Parmesan, in a large bowl. Pour into a 28 x 20-cm (11 x 8-inch) ovenproof dish and sprinkle with the Parmesan.

2 Bake in a preheated oven, 200°C (400°F), Gas Mark 6, for 15–20 minutes. Leave to cool thoroughly.

3 Cut the bake into 7-cm (3-inch) squares with a sharp knife and freeze until required for up to 3 months. Defrost thoroughly before use. Feed your dog 2–4 squares as a meal, depending on his size.

Tips'n'Tails

Parmesan can have quite a high salt content, so don't be tempted to add more than is recommended.

Pupp-eroni Pizza

A healthy, low-fat version of this popular Italian favourite. For a sweet pizza topping, try banana, pine nuts and a drizzle of honey, and reduce the cooking time accordingly.

Makes 1 paw-shaped pizza
Preparation time: 20 minutes
Cooking time: 25–30 minutes

- 125 g (4 oz) wheat- and gluten-free flour
- 1 teaspoon dried oregano
- 2 teaspoons grated low-fat Parmesan cheese
- 3 tablespoons olive oil
- 3 tablespoons cold water

For the topping:

- 5 tablespoons chopped tomatoes
- 1 teaspoon dried oregano
- handful of spinach leaves, shredded
- 2 tablespoons grated low-fat Parmesan cheese, to sprinkle

1 To make the dough, mix the flour, oregano and Parmesan in a mixing bowl. Add the olive oil and mix briefly. Add the measured water, a little at a time, until you have a firm dough. Transfer the dough to a lightly floured surface and knead lightly. Roll out three-quarters of the dough into an 18-cm (7-inch) disc. Divide the remainder of the dough into 4 and roll out each piece of dough into a 6-cm (2½-inch) disc.

2 Transfer the pizza pieces to an oiled nonstick baking sheet. Prick the dough several times with a fork. Bake in a preheated oven, 160°C (325°F), Gas Mark 3, for 10 minutes or until golden brown. Remove from the oven and set aside.

3 Mix the tomatoes, oregano and spinach in a bowl. Spread the mixture on to the pizza bases, then sprinkle with the Parmesan. Return to the oven and bake for a further 15–20 minutes.

4 Transfer to a wire rack and leave to cool thoroughly. Arrange the pieces to form the shape of a dog's paw and serve cold. Store in the refrigerator for up to 24 hours, or the freezer for up to 3 months.

Tips'n'Tails

If your dog does not have a wheat allergy, use standard plain flour instead, as the dough will be firmer and easier to roll out.

Canine's Curry with Bark-mati Rice

Does your dog drool when you eat a take-away or bring back a doggie bag from your favourite Indian restaurant? Dogs love a little spice in their life and this mild curry is a perfect option.

1 Heat the oil in a nonstick frying pan. Fry the lamb and spices for 3 minutes until lightly browned. Add the carrots, tomatoes, peas and chicken stock or water, then stir in the cornflour mixture and simmer over a medium-low heat for 5 minutes.

2 Add the spinach and rosemary and continue simmering for a further 10 minutes or until the meat is cooked through. Remove from the heat and fold in the brown rice or quinoa. Leave to cool.

3 Divide the mixture into 200-g (7-oz) portions and seal in freezer bags. Freeze until required, or up for to 3 months. Defrost a portion overnight in the refrigerator to serve.

Makes 10 portions
Preparation time: 20 minutes
Cooking time: 18–20 minutes

2 tablespoons olive oil
500 g (1 lb) minced or diced lamb
1 tablespoon fresh coriander leaves
½ teaspoon ground cumin
½ teaspoon ground turmeric
3–4 carrots, chopped
400 g (13 oz) canned chopped
 tomatoes
50 g (2 oz) fresh or frozen peas
350 ml (12 fl oz) homemade chicken
 stock or water
2 teaspoons cornflour, diluted in
 100 ml (3½ fl oz) cold water
50 g (2 oz) spinach leaves
1 rosemary sprig, finely chopped
200 g (7 oz) cooked brown basmati
 rice or quinoa

Tips'n'Tails
Substitute the lamb for chicken, heart or rabbit, if you dog prefers it, and try different types of vegetables.

Doggie Desserts

Whip up one of our delicious desserts designed to satisfy the most demanding canine sweet tooth and still be healthy.

Sweet Canine Crêpes

Your dog will leap out of bed at the merest whiff of these sweet pancakes! The seeds provide important vitamins and minerals, including vitamins B and C and potassium, while adding a little canine crunch.

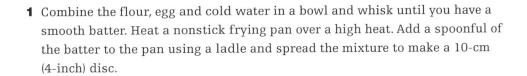

Makes 5
Preparation time: 15 minutes
Cooking time: 20–30 minutes

125 g (4 oz) wheat- and gluten-free flour
1 egg
150 ml (¼ pint) cold water
3 bananas, mashed
4 tablespoons clear honey
2 tablespoons sunflower or pumpkin seeds

1 Combine the flour, egg and cold water in a bowl and whisk until you have a smooth batter. Heat a nonstick frying pan over a high heat. Add a spoonful of the batter to the pan using a ladle and spread the mixture to make a 10-cm (4-inch) disc.

2 Fry for 2–3 minutes on each side or until the crêpe is a light golden brown. Remove from the pan and lay on kitchen paper. Repeat with the remaining batter and leave the crêpes to cool.

3 Mix the bananas, honey and seeds in a bowl and stir to combine. Divide the filling mixture between the crêpes and fold them in half. Serve in your favourite dog bowl. Store leftover crêpes in the refrigerator for up to 24 hours.

Tips'n'Tails

Sunflower seeds are rich in vitamin E and omega-6, keeping your dog's skin supple including his paw pads. Raw, unsalted sunflower seeds are beneficial for circulation and can help control cholesterol, which plays a part in conditions such as diabetes, stress, liver, kidney and cardiovascular diseases.

After-dinner Mints

Is your dog incredibly affectionate? If so, you may want to encourage him to nibble on an After-dinner Mint or two before you cuddle up together on the sofa. Mint, parsley and charcoal are bursting with bad-breath-busting ingredients and they taste good too.

Makes 30–40
Preparation time: 15 minutes
Cooking time: 25–30 minutes

250 g (8 oz) wheat- and gluten-free flour
25 g (1 oz) mint, chopped
15 g (½ oz) parsley, chopped
1 tablespoon activated charcoal
3 tablespoons olive oil
250 ml (8 fl oz) cold water, approximately

1 Combine the flour, herbs and activated charcoal in a large mixing bowl. Mix in the olive oil and add enough of the measured water, a little at a time, to make a smooth dough. Roll into 1-cm (½-inch) balls and place on a greased baking sheet.

2 Bake in a preheated oven, 180°C (350°F), Gas Mark 4, for 25–30 minutes. Remove the baking sheet from the oven and leave the After-dinner Mints to cool. Store in an airtight tin for up to 4 weeks.

Tips'n'Tails
Activated charcoal is available from good health food shops.

Canine Coolers

Keep your best friend cool on hot summer days with a refreshing canine cooler. Serve by the poochie pool or under the shade of your dog's favourite tree. Choose from the suggestions below or make up your own!

Makes 8–10
Preparation time: 15 minutes

Paw-ty Punch
100 ml (3½ fl oz) apple juice
100 ml (3½ fl oz) cranberry juice
1 teaspoon pure vanilla extract

Cheeky Chicken Cocktail
200 ml (7 fl oz) Chicken Soup (see page 40), cooled

Optional
rawhide chew sticks

1 Mix the punch ingredients together in a jug. Pour the punch, or the chicken soup, into ice-lolly moulds or ice-cube trays. If you want, replace standard 'lolly' sticks with rawhide chew sticks. Freeze until required and feed to cool canines on hot summer days.

Tips'n'Tails
Mix and match your dog's favourite flavours to make a special cocktail cooler to your own recipe. You can add low-fat yogurt to make a healthy frozen cooler. Also, you could freeze the mix in your dog's favourite interactive toy, such as a Kong, to keep him occupied.

New Bark Cheesecake

Dogs are omnivores and in the wild they would have scavenged for berries and fruits. This blueberry topping will ensure your pet receives plenty of antioxidants. If your dog is always begging for dessert, try this healthy – and famous – cheesecake!

Makes 2
Preparation time: 20 minutes, plus making cookies

400 g (13 oz) boiled swede or sweet potato, mashed
2 tablespoons peanut butter (no added salt or sugar)
1 teaspoon ground nutmeg
1 egg yolk
2 Apple and Cinnamon Lollipups made as 7-cm (3-inch) discs (see page 20)
50 g (2 oz) blueberries, plus extra to decorate
2 mint sprigs

Tips'n'Tails

Blueberries are your dog's best friend – they're packed with goodness! Most dogs love them, particularly if they are crushed a little so the sweet juice is exposed. Try adding a handful of crushed blueberries to your dog's evening meal or blending blueberries with Canine's Curry with Bark-mati rice (see page 54).

1 Combine the swede or sweet potato, peanut butter, nutmeg and egg yolk in a mixing bowl. Place the cookies on a flat serving dish. Place the cookie cutter used to cut the cookies over the top of one of them to form a mould. Half-fill the mould with the mashed swede mixture. Press down with the back of a spoon to compact.

2 Layer half the blueberries over the swede and press down again to compact. Fill the mould with the remaining swede and compact again. Carefully remove the mould and repeat with the second cheesecake. Leave to cool, then decorate each cheesecake with 3 blueberries and a mint sprig. Store any leftover cheesecakes in the refrigerator for up to 24 hours, or the freezer for up to 3 months.

Paw-lickin' Parties and Gift Ideas

At special times of the year it is easy to forget your best friend in the rush to wrap presents and bake for your family. Make this year special; bake a special treat from our selection of party favourites and paw-fect gifts.

Barkin' Birthday Cake

This moist, tasty, liver and bacon cake is bound to get the paw-ty started. Serve up slices to your canine guests and don't forget to put a piece in the doggie bag to take home!

Makes 12 portions
Preparation time: 40 minutes
Cooking time: 30–35 minutes

- 500 g (1 lb) chickens', lambs' or beef liver
- 300 ml (½ pint) semi-skimmed milk
- 500 g (1 lb) wheat- and gluten-free flour
- 3 tablespoons olive oil
- 2 eggs
- 2 tablespoons dried parsley

For the filling and frosting:

- 500 g (1 lb) low-fat cream cheese or quark
- 4 tablespoons olive oil
- 2 tablespoons honey
- 3 unsmoked bacon rashers, grilled and chopped

To decorate:

- Chicken and Tarragon Bone Biscuits (see page 17)
- birthday candles

1 Liquidize the liver and milk in a blender or food processor until smooth. Mix the flour, oil, eggs and parsley together in a mixing bowl. Fold the liver purée into the mixture and stir until it forms a smooth paste.

2 Grease 2 deep 20-cm (8-inch) sandwich tins. Divide the liver mixture equally between the tins and bake on the middle shelf of a preheated oven, 180°C (350°F), Gas Mark 4, for 30–35 minutes. Test to see if it is cooked by inserting a knife in the centre of the cake. If the knife comes out clean, the cake is cooked. Leave to cool on a wire rack.

3 To make the frosting, beat the cream cheese or quark, oil and honey together until fluffy. Place one of the cake halves upside down on a serving plate. Spread a scant half of the frosting on top and sprinkle with the chopped bacon. Place the second cake half on top of the filling, then spread the remaining frosting over the cake with a spatula.

4 Decorate with Chicken and Tarragon Bone Biscuits and candles, if desired. Store leftover cake in the refrigerator for up to 24 hours, or the freezer for up to 3 months.

Christmas Dog-erations

These festive cheese and cranberry cookies can be tied with ribbon and hung on the Christmas tree for the 12 days of Christmas – if they last that long. Leave one on a plate with a glass of milk for Santa Paws, too!

Makes 30–40
Preparation time: 30 minutes, plus hardening
Cooking time: 25–30 minutes

300 g (10 oz) wholemeal wheat- and gluten-free flour
125 ml (4 fl oz) olive oil
200 g (7 oz) low-fat Cheddar cheese, grated
75g (3 oz) dried cranberries, chopped
1 tablespoon chopped mint
100 ml (3½ oz) cold water
1 egg, beaten, to glaze

For the frosting:
250 g (8 oz) low-fat cream cheese
4 tablespoons olive oil
natural red food colouring

1 Place all the cookie ingredients, except the water, in a large bowl and mix until thoroughly combined. Slowly add the measured water to make a smooth dough. Knead the dough on a lightly floured surface until firm and then roll out to 5 mm (¼ inch) thick.

2 Cut out shapes with a festive cookie cutter. Use a skewer to make a hole approximately 5 mm (¼ inch) in diameter in each cookie, through which to thread the ribbon. Transfer the cookies to a greased baking sheet, spaced 1 cm (½ inch) apart, and brush with egg.

3 Bake the cookies in a preheated oven, 160°C (325°F), Gas Mark 3, for 25–30 minutes until firm to the touch. Remove from the oven and leave to cool and harden for 1–2 hours.

4 To make the frosting, beat together the cream cheese, oil and food colouring until fluffy. Transfer to a piping bag fitted with a fine nozzle and use to decorate the cookies. Refrigerate for 2–3 hours. Thread each cookie with a piece of ribbon approximately 15 cm (6 inches) long and hang from the tree.

Puppy Love Treats

Welcome to the family! These sweet and light natural treats are perfect for spoiling a tiny pup with a delicate digestive system.

Makes 25–30
Preparation time: 15 minutes
Cooking time: 10–15 minutes

500 g (1 lb) cooked quinoa
100g (3½ oz) plain flour
100 g (3½ oz) organic apple or banana baby food
1 egg, beaten
2 tablespoons unsalted peanuts, chopped

1 Mix the quinoa, flour, baby food and egg to bind together thoroughly.

2 Brush a heart-shaped cookie cutter with oil and place on to a greased baking sheet. Spoon a little of the mixture into the cutter and press down in an even layer. Carefully lift away the cutter. Repeat with the remainder of the quinoa mixture. Space each heart shape 1 cm (½ inch) apart, and re-oil the cutter if the mixture begins to stick. Scatter each of the cookies with the chopped peanuts, then lightly press the pieces in to the dough.

3 Bake in a preheated oven, 150°C (300°F), Gas Mark 2, for 10–15 minutes. Transfer to a wire rack to cool thoroughly. Store the cookies in a resealable plastic bag in the refrigerator and use within 5 days.

Tips'n'Tails

Check the baby food you buy does not contain onion powder, which is bad for your dog. Stuff some of the treats into the hole of a chew toy. This is great exercise for puppy teeth and the flavour of the peanuts will drive him wild.

Hallowe'en Howlers

Pamper your pet (and any other canine visitors who might turn up with the trick or treaters) with a flavourful oat, cream cheese and berry cookie. He will soon be looking forward to next year's festivities!

Makes 30–35
Preparation time: 15 minutes
Cooking time: 10–15 minutes

250 g (8 oz) oats
1 egg, beaten
125 g (4 oz) low-fat cream cheese
125 g (4 oz) strawberries, chopped
75 g (3 oz) blueberries, crushed or chopped

For the frosting:
125 g (4 oz) low-fat cream cheese

Tips'n'Tails

Oats are a good source of dietary fibre and complex carbohydrates. They make a comforting filler if feeding raw or cooked with meat and vegetables. Pour 150 g (5 oz) of oats into a saucepan and cover with boiling water. Leave to soften and cool. Mix the softened oats with meat or fish and a handful of blended vegetables to create a warming winter dinner.

1 Mix together all the ingredients in a large mixing bowl until well combined. Grease 2 baking sheets with oil.

2 Brush a decorative cookie cutter, such as a witch's hat or crescent, with oil and place on to the baking sheet. Spoon a little of the mixture into the cookie cutter and press down in an even layer. Carefully lift away the cutter. Repeat with the remainder of the mixture.

3 Bake in a preheated oven, 160°C (325°F), Gas Mark 3, for 10–15 minutes. Transfer to a wire rack to cool.

4 Place the cream cheese in a small bowl and beat with a fork to soften, then transfer to a piping bag fitted with a fine nozzle. Decorate each of the cookies. Store in an airtight container in the refrigerator for up to 3 days.

Easter Paw-rade Snacks

Watch the paw-rade go by while your dog snacks on these tasty banana and honey cookies. Banana is probably a canine's favourite fruit. Dogs love the smell, the soft texture and the sweet taste.

Makes 30–40
Preparation time: 15 minutes
Cooking time: 15–20 minutes

300 g (10 oz) wheat- and gluten-free flour
1 egg, beaten, plus extra for brushing
1 banana, mashed
2 tablespoons honey
2 drops of pure vanilla extract
3 tablespoons olive oil
2 tablespoons cold water

To decorate:
60 g (2 oz) low-fat cream cheese
1 drop of natural yellow food colouring
2 tablespoons olive oil

1 Mix all the cookie ingredients in a large mixing bowl until they come together to form a dough. Add a little more cold water, little by little, if the mixture is too dry. Knead the dough on a lightly floured surface until firm, then roll out to 5 mm (¼ inch) thick. Cut out shapes with an Easter bunny cookie cutter (or any other shaped cookie cutter as these treats are simply too good to make only at Easter).

2 Transfer the cookies to a greased baking sheet, spaced 1 cm (½ inch) apart, and brush with beaten egg. Bake in a preheated oven, 160°C (325°F), Gas Mark 3, for 15–20 minutes until firm to the touch. Remove from the oven and leave to cool on a wire rack.

3 To decorate, beat together the cream cheese, colouring and olive oil and transfer to a piping bag fitted with a fine nozzle. Pipe designs on to the Easter bunny cookies and allow to harden. Store in an airtight container in the refrigerator for up to 3 days.

Tips'n'Tails
Doughs made with wheat- and gluten-free flour are not always firm enough to be rolled out, so if your dog doesn't have a wheat or gluten allergy, use standard plain flour instead.

Paw-tune Cookies

'Canine-fucius, he say, great treats come to those who beg.' What better way to predict the future for your furry-faced friend?

Makes 12
Preparation time: 15 minutes
Cooking time: 25–30 minutes

300 g (10 oz) wheat- and gluten-free flour
100 g (3½ oz) unsalted butter
1 tablespoon ground ginger
75 ml (3 fl oz) honey
60 ml (2½ fl oz) water
12 pieces of rice paper, roughly 6 x 2.5 cm (2½ x 1 inch)

1 Combine all the ingredients, except the pieces of paper, in a large mixing bowl. Knead the mixture until it forms a firm dough. Divide the mixture into 2.5-cm (1-inch) balls.

2 Write doggie fortunes on the pieces of rice paper. Here's one to start you off: 'Canine-fucius, he say, great treats come to those who beg.' Fold the fortunes in half or quarters.

3 Roll out the dough balls into 10-cm (4-inch) discs. Place a folded fortune in the centre of each disc and fold the discs in half. Take both points of the halved discs and twist up so that the two ends meet. Press hard to stick the dough together.

4 Transfer the cookies to a nonstick baking sheet and bake in a preheated oven, 160°C (325°F), Gas Mark 3, for 25–30 minutes. Transfer to a wire rack to cool. Store in an airtight container for up to 3 weeks.

Tips'n'Tails

If you don't have rice paper use regular paper instead, but don't forget to break open the cookie and remove the fortune before giving this yummy treat to your dog!

Make-your-own Cookie Mix

Delight dog-loving friends with this healthy cookie mix, which they can bake at home. As the mixture is ready prepared, they can make cookies for their favourite pet in next to no time!

Makes 40–50
Preparation time: 15 minutes

250 g (8 oz) white wheat- and gluten-free flour
6 tablespoons dried parsley
150 g (5 oz) wholemeal wheat- and gluten-free flour
4 tablespoons sunflower seeds
4 tablespoons dried mint
100 g (3½ oz) oats or barley flakes
2 tablespoons carob powder
1 tablespoon ground cinnamon

For the packaging:
1-litre (1¾-pint) Kilner or screw-top jar
large gift card to hold recipe
ribbon
dog- or bone-shaped cookie cutter

Gift card ingredients:
150 ml (¼ pint) olive oil
1 egg, beaten, plus extra for glazing (optional)
100 g (3½ oz) Parmesan cheese or cooked boneless chicken meat, for extra-special cookies (optional)
100 ml (3½ fl oz) water

1 Wash and thoroughly dry the jar. Layer the ingredients in the jar in the following order: white flour, half the parsley, half the wholemeal flour, the remaining parsley, sunflower seeds, the remaining wholemeal flour, the mint, half the oats or barley flakes, the carob powder and then the remaining oats or barley flakes.

2 Press down with the back of a spoon to compact the mixture. Add more oats or barley if there is space left at the top of the jar. Finally, add the cinnamon to the top of the jar and seal it.

3 Punch a hole in the top left corner of the gift card and thread with the ribbon. Write the instructions below on the card and attach it to the top of the jar, together with the cookie cutter.

Gift card instructions:

Empty the contents of the jar into a large mixing bowl. Add the oil, egg and additional cheese or cooked chicken (if using). Mix until well combined. Add the water, little by little, until you have a firm dry dough. Knead the dough on a lightly floured surface and roll out to 5 mm (¼ inch) thick. Cut out dog- or bone-shaped cookies and transfer to a lightly greased baking sheet. Brush with beaten egg (if using) and bake in a preheated oven at 160°C (325°F), Gas Mark 3, for 25–30 minutes. Transfer to a wire rack and allow the cookies to cool and harden for 1–2 hours. Wash and thoroughly dry the jar, before storing your cookies in it for up to 1 week.

Box-er Chocolates

Canine chocolates beautifully gift-wrapped – perfect for Valentine's Day. Moulds for chocolate making, including heart shapes, are available from kitchenware suppliers, or improvise with an ice-cube tray.

Makes 15–25
Preparation time: 15 minutes, plus setting

250 g (8 oz) carob chips or carob bar, broken into small pieces
1 tablespoon pure vanilla extract
75 g (3 oz) pistachio nuts or peanuts, crushed

To decorate:
25 g (1 oz) blanched almonds
25 g (1 oz) glacé cherries

1 Place the carob in a heatproof glass bowl. Set the bowl over a saucepan of lightly simmering water and heat until the carob has melted. Stir in the vanilla extract and nuts. Pour into chocolate moulds or ice-cube trays and transfer to the refrigerator until set.

2 Carefully press the chocolates out of the mould or tray. Decorate each with an almond or glacé cherry. Transfer to truffle or mini cake cases and place in a small, decorated box. Cover with cling film, attach a bow and present to your favourite dog.

Tips'n'Tails

The chocolates will only keep for 5–7 days as they are made from natural ingredients, unlike commercial chocolates. Don't be tempted to substitute cocoa powder for the carob as chocolate is poisonous to dogs.

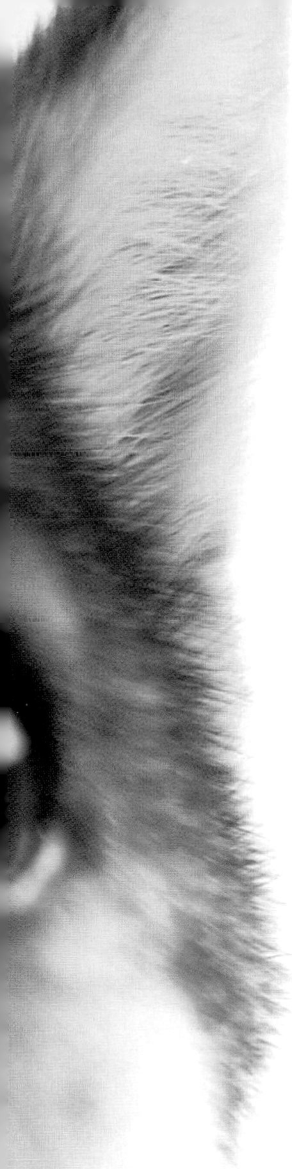

Healthy Hounds

If your dog is feeling a little under the weather or has a few pounds to lose, try making one of our healthy low-fat treats, which are guaranteed to make him sit up and beg.

Flea-fighters

Garlic is known for its health-giving properties – and also its smell! Most dogs go wild for it, but fleas seem to hate it. Feed your dog a bye-bye flea biscuit and help send those itchy little friends back to the flea circus.

Makes 40–60
Preparation time: 15 minutes
Cooking time: 20–25 minutes

250 g (8 oz) wheat- and gluten-free flour
1 teaspoon brewer's yeast
½ teaspoon chopped garlic
3 tablespoons olive oil
75 ml (3 fl oz) cold water

1 Combine the flour, brewer's yeast and garlic in a large mixing bowl. Mix in the olive oil and add the measured water, a little at a time, until you have a smooth dough.

2 Divide the mixture in two and roll one half into 1½-cm (¾-inch) balls, transfer to a greased baking sheet and flatten with the back of a fork. Shape small lumps of mixture from the other half of the dough into bone shapes and transfer to the greased baking sheet.

3 Bake in a preheated oven, 180°C (350°F), Gas Mark 4, for 20–25 minutes. Transfer to a wire rack and leave to cool. Store in an airtight container for up to 3 weeks.

Tips'n'Tails

Fleas hate garlic, so you can do a lot to help keep them at bay by introducing garlic and brewer's yeast to your dog's diet. If you want to avoid giving your dog too many treats, or if he isn't keen on the taste of garlic, mix a little into his food.

Tummy-rub Tea

The perfect tea for an upset tummy. Has your dog stolen a little too much cake? Or maybe he's just enjoyed too many treats? Feed him this bland, low-fat meal for a day or two and let him detox his way back to health.

Makes 1–2 portions
Preparation time: 20 minutes
Cooking time: 25 minutes

200 g (7 oz) boneless, skinless chicken or turkey, cooked and shredded
1 egg, hard-boiled and shelled
100 g (3½ oz) quinoa or white rice, cooked
good-quality vitamin and mineral supplement (according to the manufacturers' instructions or as directed by your vet)

Tips'n'Tails
Ask your vet to recommend the vitamin and mineral supplement and the quantity to give your dog. If your dog continues to feel unwell, begins to vomit or has diarrhoea, consult your vet as soon as possible.

1 Mix the chicken or turkey, egg, quinoa or rice and supplement in a large mixing bowl. Feed the equivalent of half your dog's normal daily food weight, or divide the mixture into smaller portions and feed little and often throughout the day. Store the mixture in the refrigerator for up to 24 hours, or freeze and defrost when required.

Pick-me-up Punch

The ultimate in health drinks. This balanced smoothie contains all the necessary vitamins and minerals to keep an active dog on the move. Mix with your dog's regular dry or wet food.

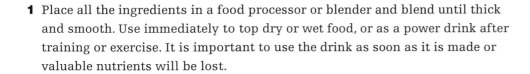

Makes 5–8 portions
Preparation time: 15 minutes

1 kiwifruit, peeled
25 g (1 oz) strawberries
25 g (1 oz) blackberries
1 banana, chopped
5 ready-to-eat dried apple rings or apricot halves
25 g (1 oz) hazelnuts or blanched almonds, chopped
25 g (1 oz) pumpkin seeds
1 tablespoon milled flaxseed
1 carrot, chopped
1 handful of spinach, rocket or alfalfa
1 tablespoon omega-3 fish oil

1 Place all the ingredients in a food processor or blender and blend until thick and smooth. Use immediately to top dry or wet food, or as a power drink after training or exercise. It is important to use the drink as soon as it is made or valuable nutrients will be lost.

Tips'n'Tails

Flaxseed is nutty and crunchy and full of omega-3 fatty acids, which are good for your dog's skin, particularly if he is prone to inflammation or dry patches. Omega-3 is also believed to help ease the symptoms of arthritis.

Fat Busters

If your dog is on a diet, a healthy and tasty dog smoothie or tidbit should hit the spot. You will soon see your furry friend skipping round the block, minus the flab.

Makes: 3–4 or 18–20 portions
Preparation time: 15 minutes
Cooking time: 20–25 minutes (Low Calorie Pleaser)

Fruity Fat Buster

- 1 banana or apple, finely sliced
- 50 g (2 oz) dried apricots, chopped
- 25 g (1 oz) dates, chopped
- 100 ml (3½ oz) low-fat live natural yogurt
- 1 teaspoon honey

Veggie Delight

- 50 g (2 oz) carrots
- 50 g (2 oz) celery
- 25 g (1 oz) spinach
- 25 g (1 oz) mangetout
- 100 ml (3½ oz) low-fat live natural yogurt

Low Calorie Pleaser

- 2 tablespoons blackstrip molasses
- 200 g (7 oz) cooked boneless and skinless turkey or salmon pieces
- 1 teaspoon dried mixed herbs
- 1 tablespoon sesame seeds

Fruity Fat Buster

Place the fruits, yogurt and honey in a small bowl and toss together until all the fruits are well covered with the yogurt and honey. Serve over regular dog food or as a snack. Makes 3–4 portions.

Veggie Delight

Blend all the ingredients in a food processor or blender on a high setting for about 20 seconds. Alternatively, chop the vegetables finely and mix with the yogurt. Serve over regular dog food or as a snack. Makes 3–4 portions.

Low Calorie Pleaser

Place the blackstrip molasses and cooked boneless and skinless turkey or salmon pieces in a bowl. Roll the turkey or salmon pieces in the molasses until well covered and transfer to a nonstick baking sheet. Sprinkle with the dried mixed herbs and sesame seeds. Place in a preheated oven, 150°C (300°F), Gas Mark 2, and cook for 20–25 minutes or until slightly crunchy. Remove from the oven and leave to cool. Transfer to an airtight container and store in the refrigerator for up to 24 hours. Makes 18–20 portions.

Index

Acknowledgements

Dedication
This book is dedicated to Alfie, my inspiration and my obsession.

Author's acknowledgements
I wish to thank everyone who helped me create PupCakes. In particular, my husband, Shadi, who tirelessly created and recreated recipes in our kitchen while I tapped away at the keyboard. Special thanks also to Ella, the Greek Goddess, who excelled in her role as canine kitchen assistant. Thanks to Fiona Robertson for her review of the recipes and general information in this book and for sharing her knowledge and expertise in canine nutrition. Special slobbery kisses go to the taste-testing team, always willing and able: Judy, Stella, Megan, Summer, Rhia, Cassie, Fiver, Jasper, Millie, Henry, Sunny, and Ben. Thanks to Jo at K9 Solutions for all her help and support and to Lynette and everyone at our Saturday morning doggie socials for trying new treats and being as excited about the book as I am. Thanks to the team at Hamlyn including Jane Donovan, Cressida Malins, Camilla Davis, Darren Southern, Joanna Farrow, Stephen Conroy and Joseph Williams for helping me make sense of my ramblings and sketchy recipes. Thanks to my family and friends for their patience and support, in particular my Mum, who is always my greatest supporter. Thanks to Selfridges in London for providing all the beautiful accessories for our doggie models.

The author and publisher would like to extend special thanks to Amelia Lowe from Paws4Walks (www.paws4walks.com), Fenella Reilly from Nuts about Mutts (www.nutsaboutmutts.co.uk) and Sarah Stewart-Richardson for their generous help in providing models. Finally thank you to our wonderful canine models – Anya, Basil, Chico, Chilli, Eeda, Eric, Freddie, Holly, Jessie, Katie, Kaya, Lady, Larry, Lily, Maggot, Meg, Nellie, Percy, Poppy, Rafiki and Tarka – without whom the book would not have been possible.

About the Canine Cookie Company
We love dogs. Our dogs are our family. They deserve the best. That's why we created the Canine Cookie Company. We bake healthy, handmade treats free from added salt, sugar, additives and preservatives. Spoil your dog, order a gourmet treat from Canine Cookie Company today! www.caninecookiecompany.co.uk

Executive editor: Jane Donavan
Editor: Camilla Davis
Executive art editor: Darren Southern
Designer: Tim Pattinson
Home Economist: Joanna Farrow
Photographer: Stephen Conroy
Production manager: Nigel Reed
Special photography: Octopus Publishing Group Ltd/Stephen Conroy
Props Stylist: Sarah Waller